STENOGRAPHER SECRETARIAL ASSISTANT (ENGLISH) MCQ

OBJECTIVE QUESTION ANSWERS

MANOJ DOLE

Digitization is the need of the time. In the future, training in industrial training institutes will need to be conducted using online internet to make training more convenient and easy. E-books containing a set of MCQ questions will be made available to the trainees as they need to be more accustomed to the multiple choice questions MCQ to prepare for the online exams taking place in their industrial training institutes.

With all these factors in mind, Mr. Manoj Madhukar Dole Instructor, Industrial Training Institute, Satara, has written books according to the new annual system and NSQF-5 syllabus. And they've created theoretical mobile apps and blogs to make training easier, and made all these educational materials available for download on the world famous websites Google Play Store, Amazon and Apple Book Store.

The books were published by Hon'ble Joint Director Shri Rajendra Ghume Saheb Regional Office of Vocational Education and Training, Pune on 9/1/2019, at this time Shri Prakash Saigavkar Saheb Principal Government Industrial Training Institute Aundh Pune, Shri Tukaram Misal Saheb Principal Govt. Q. Sanstha Satara, Shri Sachin Dhumal Saheb District Vocational Education and Training Officer Satara, Shri Yatin Pargaonkar Saheb Principal Govt. Q. Sanstha Kolhapur, Shri Vikas Teke Saheb Inspector Vocational Education and Training Regional Office Pune, Palekar Foods Products Pvt. Ltd. Entrepreneurial Chairman of Satara Mr. Nilkanthrao Palekar Saheb, Chairman of Hira Foods Mr. Ibrahim Baba Tamboli Saheb, Mrs. Shalmali Pawar Headmaster Government Technical School Center Satara and other dignitaries were present on the occasion.

Contents

Prologue

Stenographer secretarial Assistant (English) is a simple Book for ITI Engineering Course Stenographer secretarial Assistant (English) , Sem- 1 & 2, Revised NSQ F-5 Syllabus in 2022, It contains objective questions with underlined & bold correct answers MCQ covering all topics including all about safety and environment, use of Stenographer Secretarial Assistant English, computer hardware & its peripherals, CONSONANTS & ITS DIRECTION /JOINING THE CONSONANTS, long & short vowels, Describe Logograms, Grammalogues Contraction & use of 'the' /punctuation mark, Diphthong, Prepare Windows operating system on computer, finger positioning on the computer, curved hooked strokes and compound consonant, Recognize Final Hooks, Recognize Final Hooks, List the prefixes, List the suffixes, MS-Excel, Label the office layout, file & prepare MS-Power point, Demonstrate MS-PowerPoint Presentation, Create E-Mail ID, correspondence through mail, filling up online forms and documents for registration, all types of letters, notice, agenda, minutes, reports, circular & memorandum and lots more.

We add new question answers with each new version. Please email us in case of any errors/omissions. This is arguably the largest and best e-Book for All engineering multiple choice questions and answers.

As a student you can use it for your exam prep. This e-Book is also useful for professors to refresh material.

Foreword

Vocational education and training is imparted through the Department of Vocational Education and Training through the Department of Business Education and Business Practical to supply multi-skilled artisans in line with the rapidly growing demand in the industrial sector in the 21st century. All the occupations within the institutions are important, as the trainees from these occupations develop multi-skills as per the demands of the industry.

with the noble intention of making available MCQ e-books suitable for all businesses, considering that all the examinations in all the industries in the industrial sector are conducted online and include MCQ method questions. Mr. Manoj Madhukar Dole has written a very good e-book on MCQ method as per the new annual syllabus. This e-book will definitely be a guide for all the trainees, trainee candidates, training instructors and others concerned.

The author of the book is Mr. Manoj Madhukar Dole, Instructor Gov. ITI Satara has 17 years of training experience. Written as a new annual pattern, this e-book incorporates modern digital QR Code technology to understand the layout, simple language, and simple syntax, diagrams and videos for each subject. So I am sure that this e-book will definitely be useful for in-depth study and exam practice. The work they have done is certainly commendable.

Mr. Tukaram Misal
Principal Government Industrial Training Institute Satara.

Preface

DGET New Delhi and CSTARI Kolkata have been implementing an annual pattern for all businesses in ITI since the August 2018 session. The examination system will also be changed and it will be online from this year and since all the questions are of Objective Type (MCQ), the trainees are in dire need of in-depth study. It is with this in mind that we are delighted to present the books based on the old NIMI pattern and a complete overview of the new annual pattern, and we hope that these books will be a guide for all business directors and trainees. Is.

For writing these books, Johar Awate Saheb, Principal of ITI Akluj. Former Principal of ITI Satara Saigavkar Saheb, Assistant Director Shri Chandrakant Dhekne Saheb Regional Office of Vocational Education and Training, Pune, District Vocational Education and Training Officer Sachin Dhumal Saheb and Headmaster Government Technical School Kendra Shalmali Pawar Madam and son Adhiraj Dole, mother Kusum Dole, I am very grateful to my father Madhukar Dole and wife Ashwini Dole for their special guidance and cooperation from time to time.

Also, in a very short period of time, the book was reviewed by Shri Rajendra Ghume Saheb, Joint Director, Vocational Education and Training Regional Office, Pune, for his invaluable time in publishing the book. I am sincerely grateful for their feedback.

I am grateful to the Instructor of ITI Satara for there continuous support from the very beginning of writing the book.

From this book, I consider myself blessed to have shared my thoughts on e-learning with you. I will not claim that this book is perfect, because considering the perfection, this book is an attempt and is in its infancy. They will be valuable for improvement if they are tested and suggested.

Manoj Dole
Dated 9/1/2019

Acknowledgements

The industrial training and theoretical examination system of our industrial training institutes and these changes have been accepted by the craft instructors and the trainees. Theoretical examinations conducted in your industrial training institutes are also conducted online. Since these examinations are of multiple choice MCQ method, the trainees will need to get more practice of such questions.

With all these considerations in mind, Mr. Manoj Madhukar, Director, Dole Crafts, Katari Industrial Training Institute, Satara, has done a thorough study and with his diligent work and added his keen intellect, according to the new annual system and NSQF-5 syllabus, e-book of Katari and other machine trades. -Book) and they have created mobile apps and blogs on theoretical topics to make training easier and have made all these educational materials available for download on the world famous websites Google Play Store, Amazon and Apple Book Store. Training has been made easier by creating a print version and using advanced techniques like QR Code.

All these educational materials will definitely be a guide for all the trainees for in-depth study and for the craft instructors and other concerned who are imparting vocational training.

CHAPTER ONE

Stenographer Secretarial Assistant (English) MCQ

01] How the consonants except (W & Y] are formed?

a] By Simplest geometrical diagrams,

b] By design,

c] By lines only,

d] By Curves only.

02] Consonants P,B,T,D,CH, J, K,G are ....

a] Continuants,

b] explodents,

c] Liquids,

d] Coalescents.

03]Consonants F, V, TH, S, Z, SH, ZH are......

a] continuants,

b] explodents,

c] Liquids,

d] Coalescents.

04] Consonants M, N, NG are.....

a] continuants,

b] explodents,

c] Nasals,

d] Coalescents.

05] Consonants L, R(up/Down] are....

a] continuents,

b] explodents,

c] Liquids,

d] Coalescents.

06] Consonants W, Y, H(UP/down] are...

a] continuents,

b] explodents,

c] Liquids,

d] Coalescents.

07] Consonants H(UP/down] are...

a] continuents,

b] explodents,

c] Liquids,

d] Aspirates.

08] Who invented the system of shorthand?

a] John Baired,

b] Charles Babbage,

c] Henry Mill,

D] Emily Smith.

09]When the system of shorthand was invented?

a] In 1836,

b] In 1837,

c] In 1838,

d] In 1835.

10] What is the other name of Shorthand system?

a] Phonography,

b] Typography,

c] Dictation,

d] Stenographer.

11]The consonants written from top downwards are called.....

a] upstrokes,

b] Downstrokes,

c] Horizontals,

d] alphabets.

12] The consonants written from down to top are called.....

a] upstrokes ,

b] Downstrokes,

c] Horizontals,

d] alphabets.

13] The consonants written from left to right are called.....

a] upstrokes ,

b] Downstrokes,

c] Horizontals,

d] alphabets.

14] The Standard size of the consonants should be.... Of an inch.

a] two three ,

b] one sixth ,

c] one fifth ,

d] two fourth.

15] There are ....total alphabets in shorthand.

a] 15,

b] 24,

c] 26,

D] 28

Chapter No. 2
THE VOWELS

16] The heavy vowels are...... vowels.

a] Long,

b] Short,

c] dark ,

d] faint.

17] The light vowels are......vowels.

a] Long,

b] Short,

c] Dark,

d] Faint.

18]If the mouth passage is left so open as not to cause audible friction, and voiced breadth is sent through it we have.......a

a] diphthong,

b] Vowel,

c] diphone,

d] triphone.

19] The vowel places are counted from.............

a] Top downward,

b] Down to top,

c] From where stroke begins,

d] Horizontals.

20] When the vowel comes first and then consonant, such vowels are called....

a] preceding,

b] Following,

c] Intervening,

d] both-preceding and following.

21] When the vowel comes after the consonant, such vowels are called....

a] Preceding,

b] Following,

c] Intervening,

d] both-preceding and following.

22] When the vowel comes before and after the consonant, such vowels are called....

a] Preceding,

b] Following,

c] Intervening,

d] both-preceding and following.

23] The long vowels are represented by......

a] Heavy dot & dash,

b] Light dot & dash,

c] Circles,

d] Loops.

24] The..............are called, first place, second place and third place respectively.

a] Vowels,

b] Diphthongs,

c] triphones,

d] Circles.

25]The placement of vowels in case of horizontals are given......the consonant.

a] Before and after ,

b] Above and below,

c] Right and left,

d] Left and right.

Chapter No.3

INTERVENING VOWELS AND POSITION

26] What are Grammalogues?

a] frequently occurring words

b] Some time occurring words,

c] Small words,

d] Other.

27] What are intervening vowels? The vowels.....

a] Between two consonants,

b] Before the consonants,

c] After the consonant,

d] other.

28] The third place vowel occure after the first consonant is written......

a] Before the second stroke,

b] Before the second stroke at the end,

c] Before the first stroke,

d] Other.

29] When the first sounded vowel in a word is a first place vowel, the outline is written in ----position.

a] Second,

b] Third,

c] First,

d] Other.

30] When the first sounded vowel in a word is a second place vowel, the outline is written in ----position.

a] Second,

b] Third,

c] First,

d] Other.

31] When the first sounded vowel in a word is a third place vowel, the outline is written in ----position.

a] Second,

b] Third,

c] First,

d] Other.

32] The full stop is written in shorthand by......

a] Full stop,

b] Small cross,

c] Small circle,

d] Other.

33] The note of interrogation is represented in shorthand by......

a] Full stop,

b] Small cross,

c] Question mark and cross,

d] Other.

34] The note of exclamation is represented in shorthand by......

a] Full stop,

b] Exclamatory sign and a cross,

c] Question mark and cross,

d] Other.

35] The horizontal consonants are written in the ....position.

a] Second,

b] Third,

c] First,

d] Other.

Chapter No.4

ALTERNATIVE SIGNS FOR R AND H

36] The consonant R is provided with ....forms.

a] Three,

b] Four,
c] Five,
d] two.
37] If the initial R is preceded by a vowel, it is written...............
a] Upward,
b] downward,
c] Any form,
d] Other.
38] If the R consonant is followed a vowel finally, it is written..............
a] Upward,
b] downward,
c] Any form,
d] Other.
39] Middle R is always written.........
a] Upward,
b] downward,
c] Any form,
d] Other.
40] Consonant H is provided with............forms.
a] Three,
b] Four,
c] Five,
d] two.
41] The............form of H is most commonly used.
a] Upward,
b] downward,
c] Any form,
d] Other.
42] The downward form of H is used when H stands alone or it is followed by...........
a] PB,
b] FV,
c] K,G,
d] M,N.

Chapter No.5.

Dipthongs

43] ....is a union of two vowels sounds in one syllable.
a] Triphone,

b] Dipthong,
c] Diphone,
d] Other answer
44] ......Diphthongs are placed at First Place of consonants.
a] I, OI,
b] OW, U ,
c] Ah, I ,
d] Other answer.
45] . ...Diphthongs are placed at Third Place of consonants.
a] I, OI,
b] OW, U ,
c] Ah, I ,
d] Other answer.
46] Dipthongs can be joined................
a] Initially,
b] Medially,
c] Previously,
d] Finally.
47] ....is a union of three vowels sounds in one syllable.
a] Triphone,
b] Diphthong,
c] Diphone,
d] Other answer
48] ......Triphones are placed at First Place of consonants.
a] I & OI with any vowel,
b] OW &U with any vowel
c] I & E with any vowel,
d] Other answer.
49] . . ..Triphones are placed at First Place of consonants.
a] I & OI with any vowel,
b] OW &U with any vowel
c] I & E with any vowel,
d] Other answer.
50] The initial sound of ....before K,G,M,R-up/down is abbreviated.
a] M,
b] W,
c] L,
d] S

Chapter No. 6.

Phraseography

51] ....is a writing of two or more words without lifiting a pen.mOo

a] Phraseography,

b] Intersections,

c] Contractions,

d] Other answer.

52] The practice of ....writing increases speed of the shorthand writer.

a] English,

b] Phrase,

c] Consonant,

d] Other answer.

53] The ....word form of a phraseogram occupy the position of a phrase.

a] Last,

b] Middle,

c] First,

d] Other answer.

4] The outline can be made legible by inserting the...........

a] diphthong,

b] triphone,

c] Vowel,

d] Other.

CHAPTER NO. 07

54] A small circle used initially represents ......only.

a] z,

b] s,

c] s or z ,

d] Other answer.

55] A small circle finally used represents........

a] z,

b] s,

c] s or z ,

d] Other answer.

56] The ....circle is always read first.

a] Final,

b] Medial,

c] Initial,

d] Other answer

57] The ....circle is always read last.

a] Final,

b] Medial,

c] Final,

d] Other answer

58] The stroke L, immediately preceding or following a circle attached to a curve is in the.................

a] Same direction a circle,

b] Same direction as stroke,

c] Same direction as phrase,

d] Other

59] circle S, may be added to....

a] Small circle,

b] Large circle,

c] Stroke logogram,

d] Other answer.

60] Where the stroke S is written initially in the root word, it is retained in...........

a] Phrases,

b] Compounds and derivatives,

c] Strokes and logograms,

d] Other answer.

CHAPTER NO. 08
STROKES S AND Z

61] When a vowel precedes initial S or follows final S or Z these consonants are.....

a] Halved,

b] Fully written,

c] Dropped,

d] Other answer.

62] When initial S is immediately followed by a vowel and another....

a] sw and ss,

b] s or z,

c] Consonant and phrase,

d] Other answer.

63] The stroke S or Z must be written in full when final syllable -ous is preceded by.......

a] vowel,

b] triphone,

c] Diphthong,

d] Diaphone.

64] The stroke S or Z must be written in full when there is............word.

a] Halving,

b] Doubling,

c] Compound,

d] Abbreviated.

65] The stroke S or Z must be written in full when...........

a] There is a circle,

b] Vowel precedes initial s or follows final s or z,

c] Consonant precedes initial s,

d] Consonant follows final s or z.

CHAPTER NO. 9

LARGE CIRCLES SW AND SS OR SZ.

66] A large circle initially represents.........

a] s circle,

b] st loop,

c] sw circle,

d] ss or sz circle.

67] A large circle medially or finally represents the sound of...........with an intervening vowel.

a] s ,

b] st ,

c] sw ,

d] ss

68] Where the root word ends with stroke S, the plural, possessive, or the third person singular is formed by the use of..........

a] str loop finally,

b] sw circle,

c] ses circle,

d] s circle.

69] Large circle in phraseography is used as..........

a] sw and s,

b] s and s,

c] Consonant and s,

d] Other answer.

70] The final s can be added after...........

a] Small circle,

b] Large circle,

c] Contraction,

d] Other answer.

71] ....circle written with the same motion as the circle s, represents the double consonant.

a] a large final ,

b] A large medial,

c] A large initial,

d] Other answer.

CHAPTER NO. 10.
LOOP ST AND STR.

72] A small loop represents............

a] st,

b] str,

c] sw,

d] ss or sz

73] A large loop represents............

a] st,

b] str,

c] sw,

d] ss or sz

74] The ....loop is used initially, medially and finally.

a] str,

b] st,

c] ss or sz,

d] sw

75] The ....loop is used medially and finally but not initially.

a] str,

b] st,

c] ss or sz,

d] sw

76] The ST loop is employed finally to represent the sound of....... also.

a] zd,

b] sw,

c] str,
d] Other answer.
77] When a strongly sounded vowel occurs ...cannot be used.
a] str,
b] st,
c] ss or sz,
d] sw
78] When a vowel follows finally ...cannot be used.
a] ses,
b] st,
c] ss or sz,
d] sw

CHAPTER NO. 11.
INITIAL HOOKS TO STRAIGHT STROKES AND CURVES.

79]A small initial hook written with the Right motion adds.......... to the straight strokes.
a] N,
b] R,
c] L,
d] Other answer
80] A large initial hook written with the Right motion adds.......... to the straight strokes.
a] N,
b] R,
c] L,
d] Other answer
81] The hooked signs are called by their.............
a] Personal names,
b] Professional names,
c] Syllabic names,
d] Other answer.
82] A small initial hook adds ....to the curved consonant.
a] N,
b] R,
c] L,
d] Other answer
83] A large initial hook adds ....to the curved consonant.
a] N,

b] R,

c] L,

d] Other answer

84]............is always written upward.

a] shr,

b] shl,

c] fl,

d] vl

85] ....with small initial hook represents the sound of ng-gr, ng-kr.

a] mg,

b] nk,

c] ng,

d] Other answer.

CHAPTER NO. 12.
ALTERNATIVE FORMS.

86] When standing alone, if a vowel precedes, the left curves are written in ....

a] Alternative form,

b] halved form,

c] Double form,

d] Regular form

87] When standing alone, if vowel does not precede, the left curves are written in ....

a] Alternative form,

b] halved form,

c] Double form,

d] Regular form

88] When joined to another stroke................form is used.

a] Alternative form,

b] Either form,

c] Double form,

d] Regular form

89] After straight upstrokes and horizontals............form is used.

a] Alternative form,

b] Either form,

c] Double form,

d] Regular form

90] Intervening vowel is indicated by..............

a] Dot and dash,
b] Cross and tick,
c] Circle and dash,
d] Other answer.
91] while indicating intervening dot vowel, the ....is used.
a] Dash,
b] Cross,
c] Circle
d] Other answer.

CHAPT. NO. 35
INTERSECTIONS

92] Intersections are used for writing............
a] Only outlines
b] Only strokes
c] Name of persons and organisations
d] Phrases.
93]The Intersection method is used of writing...........................
a] separately,
b] In close proximity,
c] far,
d] Other.
94] P is intersected to write as................
a] Policy,
b] Party,
c] Public,
d] Property
95] PR is intersected to represent as....................
a] proprietor
b] Press,
c] Professor,
d] Prime
96] B is intersected to represent as....................
a] Bank, bill
b] Be, bye,
c] Bureau, but,
d] Body, base
97] T is intersected to represent as....................
a] Tension,

b] Technical,
c] Attention,
d] Telegram
98] D is intersected to represent as....................
a] Divide,
b] Deploy,
c] Delay,
d] Department
99] CH is intersected to represent as....................
a] Change,
b] Chancery,
c] Chain,
d] Cheer
100] J is intersected to represent as....................
a] Jump,
b] Journal,
c] Journey,
d] Jar
101] K is intersected to represent as....................
a] Company,
b] Camel,
c] Care,
d] Cotton
102] KR is intersected to represent as....................
a] colonel
b] Kernel
c] Create
d] Care
103] G is intersected to represent as....................
a] Group
b] Guardian,
c] Government,
d] Grain
104] F is intersected to represent as....................
a] Fame,
b] Farm,
c] Form,
d] Frame

105] V is intersected to represent as...................
a] Vitamin,
b] Valutation,
c] Visitation,
d] Other.
106] TH is intersected to represent as...................
a] month,
b] Theory,
c] Thirsty,
d] Thursday
107] S is intersected to represent as...................
a] situation,
b] Seem,
c] Society,
d] Social
108] M is intersected to represent as...................
a] Money,
b] Major,
c] Meter,
d] Margin
109] N is intersected to represent as...................
a] Near,
b] Not,
c] Navy,
d] National
110] L is intersected to represent as...................
a] Legal
b] Liberal,
c] Limit,
d] Loyal
111] R (up] is intersected to represent as...................
a] Arrange
b] Require,
c] Rare,
d] Record
112] R (down] is intersected to represent as...................
a] Arrange,
b] Require,

c] Rare,
d] Record
113] SR is intersected to represent as...................
a] Conspiracy,
b] Serial,
c] Conservative,
d] serial

CHAPT. NO. 34
ADVANCED PHRASEOGRAPHY

114] A large circle is used as .... in phrases.
a] as-W,
b] As we,
c] As well,
d] Other.
115] ST loop is used as ....in phrases.
a] Text,
b] First,
c] Vest,
d] Other
116] Doubling principle is used as............... in phraseography.
a] tr,dr,
b] their, there,
c] thr,
d] ture
117] ....principle is used for negative use in phrases.
a] Doubling,
b] Halving,
c] Suffix,
d] Prefix

CHAPT. NO. 33.
SPECIAL CONTRACTIONS

118] Some contractions are formed by..........
a] Words,
b] Phrases,
c] With first two or three strokes,
d] Other
119] Some contractions are formed by..........
a] Words,

b] Phrases,
c] Medial omission,
d] Other
120] Some contractions are formed by..........
a] Words,
b] Phrases,
c] Logograms,
d] Other
121] Some contractions are formed by..........
a] Words,
b] Phrases,
c] Intersections,
d] Other

CHAPT. NO. 31.
NOTE TAKING AND TRANSCRIPTIONS.

122] While writing on a desk or a table.................
a] Put a finger below page in order to open up quickly.
b] Tear off pages in order to write over them,
c] Use a ruled note book in order to write in shorthand.,
d] Answer other than these.
123] In a phraseography, necessity of vowels are................
a] Avoided,
b] reduced to a minimum,
c] Inserted where necessary,
d] Other answer.
124] The knowledge of .... is important for note taking.
a] Outlines,
b] contracted forms,
c] Translation,
d] Other answer.
125] If several outlines are wrongly written then.............
a] Practice again,
b] Reduce the speed,
c] Study hard,
d] Other answer.
126] The regular practice will make your writing.....
a] Smooth,
b] Instinctive,

c] Legible,
d] Other answer.
127] The varied dictation can increase..............
a] Your writing power,
b] Your vocabulary,
c] Your speed writing,
d] Other.
128] The pen should be held only with the............... pressure.
a] Heavy,
b] Light,
c] Moderate,
d] Other.
129] Distinguishing vowels should be inserted in order to................
a] Recognize same outlines,
b] Distinguish same outlines,
c] To write full outlines
d] Other

CHAPTER NO. 32
ESSENTIAL VOWELS.

130] Vowels should be inserted where there is..........
a] Unknown contexts,
b] Phrases,
c] Grammalogues,
d] Other.
131] The vowels must be inserted where the..............
a] The contractions to be written,
b] Subject matter is unknown,
c] Advance outlines,
d] Other
132] In a single stroke, outlines having initial and final vowels, the............ vowels should be inserted.
a] Initial,
b] Final,
c] Medial,
d] Other.
133] The outline can be made legible by inserting the.............
a] diphthong
b] Triphone,

c] Vowel,

d] Other.

134] The Note Taking means.............

a] Writing of dictation in shorthand,

b] Writing of words only,

c] Writing of trade theory,

d] Other than this.

135] The position of writing must be............

a] Simple,

b] Erect,

c] As per writers` convenience.

d] Other.

136] In practising the rules, it is most important to study.............

a] Weekly,

b] Monthly,

c] Quarterly,

d] Daily

137] The study of shorthand can be covered by taking down.............

a] Translation,

b] Dictation,

c] Practice of theory,

d] All alternatives.

CHAPTER NO. 15.
THE CIRCLES AND LOOPS TO FINAL HOOKS.

138] The sound of N can be added to the final attachments by.............

a] Writing consonant with them,

b] By way of omission,

c] By writing final attachment on the same side as hook,

d] By writing attachments inside the hook.

139] The final small circle cannot be added to mix f or v sound finally to it as in case of mixing N sound, if we want them to add sound f or v, we have to

a] Write circle inside the hook,

b] Write full consonant of f/v then write circle,

c] Avoid attaching circle,

d] Other answer.

140] The light sound of Ns after a curve is expressed by.............

a] NG and S,

b] H and S,

c] M and S,

d] Other answer.

141] The circle Ns or Nz occur medially then..........

a] Both letters must be shown,

b] <u>Both letters must be abbreviated</u>,

c] Some letters must be avoided,

d] Other answer.

CHAPTER NO. 16
THE SHUN HOOK

142] The hook -shun is written to curves.............

a] Outside angles,

b] <u>Inside curves</u>,

c] Written by stroke,

d] Another answer

143] The hook –shun is written to straight strokes with initial attachment on the.....

a] Same side of attachment,

b] <u>On opposite side of attachment</u>,

c] Below attachment,

d] Other answer.

144] The –shun hook is written to K and G while following curves.....

a] <u>With both motions to keep horizontals straight</u>.

b] With left motion for convenience in writing.

c] With right motion,

d] Other answer.

145] The –shun hook is written to straight strokes except T,D & J is written......

a] As per convenience,

b] On the same side of last vowel,

c] <u>On the opposite side of first vowel</u>,

d] On the opposite side of last vowel.

146] The –shun hook is written to T, D & J without initial attachment...........

a] <u>On the right side</u>,

b] On the left side,

c] On both sides,

d] Other answer.

147] The –shun hook is written to the consonants following the circle S or Ns.........

a] On the same side as circle,

b] On the side opposite to the circle,

c] Below the circle,

d] Other answer.

148] The –shun hook is written finally to all consonants..........

a] With any motion,

b] As per convenience,

c] To show punctuation,

d] Other answer.

149] . The –shun hook is written medially to all consonants..........

a] With any motion,

b] As per convenience,

c] Cannot use medially,

d] Other answer.

CHAPTER NO. 17.
THE ASPIRATE

150] The upward form of H is............used.

a] Initially,

b] Finally,

c] Most commonly,

d] Other answer.

151] The downward form of H is used when it is ....

a] Followed by a horizontal,

b] Preceded by a vowel,

d] Other answer.

152] Tick H is used initially to ....

a] f, v, t

b] m, l, r

c] r (down], w, y

d] Other answer.

153] The dot H is used as..........

a] Consonant initially,

b] Consonant finally,

c] An alternative to stroke medially,

d] Other answer.

154] The ....consonant is called aspirate.

a] k

b] ch,

c] h,

d] v

CHAPTER NO. 18.

UP AND DOWN L AND SH

155] Consonant R is written downward initially, when..............

a] It is followed by a vowel,

b] It is preceded by a vowel,

c] If there is diphthong,

d] Other answer.

156] R is written downward finally, when..............

a]It is followed by a vowel,

b] It is preceded by a vowel,

c] If there is a vowel finally,

d] Other answer.

157] Medial R is written upward, when..............

a]It is followed by a vowel,

b] It is preceded by a vowel,

c] If we need good joining,

d] Other answer.

158]Medial R is always written upward..............

a] initially,

b] Finally,

c] Medially,

d] Other answer.

159] Without the sense of vowel, diphthong, consonant R is written sometimes upward and downward for.........

a] An easier outline,

b] Contractions,

c] For special nowns,

d] Other answers.

CHAPTER NO. 19.

Upward and Downward L and SH.

160] The...........form of L is most commonly written.

a] Downward,

b] upward,

c] Both forms,

d] Other answer.

161] When immediately preceding or following a circle which is attached to a curve, the L is written...........

a] Downward,

b] upward,

c] Both directions,

d] As per direction of the circle.

162] The L is written finally after........

a] f,v

b] n, ng

c] n, ng

d] Other answer.

163] Initial L is written down ward when it is.......

a] Preceded by a triphone

b] Followed by a consonant

c] Preceded by a vowel & followed by a horizontal

d] Other answer

164] After F,V & SK or a straight up stroke, Final L is written .... when followed by a vowel.

a] Up word

b] Downward

c] With any motion

d] Other answer

165] After F, V & SK or a straight up stroke, Final is written .... when not followed by a vowel.

a] Up word

b] Downward

c] With any motion

d] Other answer.

166]......... L generally written upward.

a] Initial

b] Final

c] Medial

d] Other answer

167] Stroke SH, when following a straight down stroke having an initial attachment is written........ To the initial attachment.

a] Left side

b] Right side

c] opposite

d] With up & downward directions.

CHAPTER NO. 20.

COMPOUND CONSONANTS.

168] A large initial hook adds ....to K and G makes large hook initially.

a] M,

b] w,

c] L,

d] Other answer.

169] A large initial hook to L consonant represents ....

a] W,

b] tion,

c] WH,

d] Other answer.

170] The L consonant is thickened for the addition of...........

a] er,

b] tr,

c] dr,

d] ture

171] The R consonant is thickened for the addition of...........

a] er,

b] tr,

c] dr,

d] ture

172] The addition of P or B to ....can create combine consonant.

a] v,

b] L,

c] M,

d] Other answer.

173] The aspirate is added to W by.............hook.

a] Adding,

b] Enlarging,

c] Reducing,

d] Other answer.

174] The form WL and WHL is written when ....to initial W.

a] Vowel precedes,

b] Vowel follows,

c] Diphthong precedes,

d] Other answer.

175] Initial hooks to L are always...........

a] read last,

b] read first,

c] Read medially,

d] Other answer.

CHAPTER NO. 21.
VOWEL INDICATION.

176] The Initial vowel requires............

a] The use of initial stroke,

b] The insertion of vowel,

c] The attachment of the consonant,

d] Initial attachment of hooks or loops.

177] Which is the word below comes in the group of initial vowel implied.......

a] Wear,

b] Tasty,

c] Pen,

d] Along.

178] Which is the word below comes in the group of initial consonant implied.......

a] Asleep,

b] Awake,

c] Defy,

d] less

179] which is the word below comes in the group of final consonant implied.......

a] Fall,

b] Aware,

c] Sorry,

d] Fall

180] Initial vowel requires the use of an initial stroke in order to..........

a] Give a place for the vowel sign,

b] Give a place for the final consonant,

c] To represent word in brifest form,

d] Other answer.

181] An initial or a final vowel may frequently be indicated by the form written for the...........

a] Initial or final triphone,

b] Initial or final consonant,

c] Initial or final attachment,

d] Other answer.

CAPTER NO. – 28.

SUFFIX & TERMINATIONS.

182] Instead of Stroke –ing, the ---------- is used.

a] Comma

b] Dot

c] Dash

d] Other answer

183] –Ality, -ility, -arity is used by ---------- the stroke.

a] Intersecting

b] Terminating

C] Disjoining

d] Other answer

184] The disjoined J stroke represents ----------

a] Journal

b] General

c] logical-ly

d] Other answer

185] –Ment is expressed by ----------

a] MT

b] NT

c] NGT

d] Other answer

186] The disjoined MNT represents ----------

a] Mental-ly-ity

b] Ment

C] NGT

d] Other answer

187] –Ly is represented by ----------joined or disjoined.

a] L

b] N

c] NG

d] SH

188] Joined or disjoined SH express -----------

a] –ship

b] Sheep

c] Shift

d] Other answer

189] The disjoined FS stroke expresses ----------

a] –lousiness

b] –fullness

c] Facility

d] Other answer

190] The disjoined LS stroke expresses ----------

a] –lessness

b] –fullness

c] Leisure

d] Other answer

191] W stroke halved is expressed in joining ----------

a] –word

b] When

c] Would

d] Other answer

192] Y stroke halved is expressed in joining ----------

a] –yatch

b] –yield

c] –yard

d] Other answer

CHPTER NO. 22.
THE HALVING PRINCIPLE

193] The Halving a stroke indicates the addition of...............

a]M, N, NG ,

b] T or D,

c] L & SH,

d] H, G

194] Without any attachment finally or without any Diphthong, the light stroke is halved for............only.

a] D,

b] T,

c] M,

d] Ng.

195] Without any attachment finally or without any Diphthong, the heavy stroke is halved for............only.

a] D,

b] T,

c] M,

d] Ng.

196] Vowel signs to halved forms are read.............

a] Next to the primary stroke,

b] Before the stroke,

c] As per convenience in reading,

d] Other answer.

197] A halved length H, when not joined to another stroke is always written..............

a] Downward,

b] Either motion,

c] upward ,

d] Other answer.

198] The half length ....is never written.

a] H,

b] T or D,

c] R(up],

d] Other answer.

199] The halving principle is not applied...............

a] When a word ends with a vowel,

b] When word ends with triphone,

c] When a word ends with diphthong,

d] Other answer.

200] The half length forms should not be written................to show vowels.

a] Through the line,

b] On the line,

c] Above the line,

d] Other answer.

CHAPTER NO. 23.

The Halving principle sec. II

201] The strokes M, N, L & R are halved and thickened for the addition of.............

a] T or D,

b] –lerd, -rerd etc.,

c] H, CH,

d] Other answer.

202] The thickened LD/ RD are not used when ....it.

a] Vowel comes between,

b] Vowel comes before,

c] Vowel follows,

d] Other answer.

203] MP/ MB may be halved when..............

a] Only finally hooked,

b] Only initially hooked,

c] Both initially and finally hooked,

d] Other answer.

204] RT is generally written...........

a] Downward,

b] As per convenience,

c] upward,

d] Without halving.

205] The halving ST may be written downward or upward after.............

a] T/D,

b] Horizontal,

c]- shun,

d] F/V hook

206] The stroke of unequal length must not be joined unless............

a] There is an angle at the point of junction,

b] There is good quality of joining,

c] As per convenience,

d] Other answer.

207] The stroke of unequal length must not be joined unless............

a] There is inequality of length,

b] There is good quality of joining,

c] As per convenience,

d] Other answer.

208] The half length T or D is always disjoined when immediately following Strokes..............

a] M, N, NG,

b] R, L,

c] K, G,

d] K, G, M, N
209] The halving principle is used in phraseography to represent............
a] Do not, word & would,
b] P, B, T, D,
c] L, R, H, V,
d] K, G, M, N

CHAPTER NO :-24
Suffix and Terminations

210] Instead of stroke –ing, the .... is used.
a] comma,
b] Dot,
c] Dash,
d] Other answer,
211] -Ality, -ility, -arity is used by ....the stroke.
a] Intersecting,
b] Terminating,
c] Dis-joining,
d] Other answer.
212] The disjoined J stroke represents...............
a] Journal,
b] General,
c] logical-ly,
d] Other answer,
213]-Ment is expressed by............
a] MT,
b] NT,
c] NGT,
d] Other answer,
214] The disjoined MNT represents.............
a] mental-ly-ity,
b] Ment,
c] NGT,
d] Other answer,
215] -Ly is represented by ....Joined.
a] L,
b] N,
c] NG,
d] SH,

216] Joined or disjoined SH express..............

a] -ship,

b] Sleep,

c] Shift,

d] Other answer,

217] The disjoined FS stroke express...........

a]-lousiness,

b]-fulness,

c] Facility,

d] Other answer,

218] The disjoined LS stroke express...........

a]-lessness,

b] Fullness,

c] Leisure,

d] Other answer,

219] W stroke halved is expressed in joining.............

a] -word ,

b] When,

c] Would,

d] Other answer,

220] Y stroke halved is expressed in joining.............

a] -yatch,

b] –yield,

c] –yard,

d] Other answer,

221] In Microsoft excel file is saved in ....format.

A] .mp3

B] .doc

C] .xls

D] .mpeg

222] In Microsoft excel DAVERAGE fuction is used for......

A] Counts the cells that contain numbers in a database

B] Returns the average of selected database entries

C] Extracts from a database a single record that matches the specified criteria

D] Returns the minimum value from selected database entries

223] In Microsoft excel DCOUNT fuction is used for......

A] Counts the cells that contain numbers in a database

B] Returns the average of selected database entries

C] Extracts from a database a single record that matches the specified criteria

D] Returns the minimum value from selected database entries

224] Function in Microsoft excel Extracts from a database a single record that matches the specified criteria...

A] DGET

B] DMAX

C] DMIN

D] DPRODUCT

225] Function in Microsoft excel Returns the maximum value from selected database entries.

A] DGET

B] DMAX

C] DMIN

D] DPRODUCT

226] Function in Microsoft excel Returns the minimum value from selected database entries

A] DGET

B] DMAX

C] DMIN

D] DPRODUCT

227] Function in Microsoft excel Multiplies the values in a particular field of records that match the criteria in a database

A] DGET

B] DMAX

C] DMIN

D] DPRODUCT

228] In Microsoft excel which function Estimates the standard deviation based on a sample of selected database entries

A] DSTDEV

B] DSTDEVP

C] DSUM

D] DVAR

229] In Microsoft excel which function Calculates the standard deviation based on the entire population of selected database entries

A] DSTDEV

B] DSTDEVP

C] DSUM

D] DVAR

230] In Microsoft excel which function Adds the numbers in the field column of records in the database that match the criteria

A] DSTDEV

B] DSTDEVP

C] DSUM

D] DVAR

230] In Microsoft excel which function Estimates variance based on a sample from selected database entries

A] DSTDEV

B] DSTDEVP

C] DSUM

D] DVAR

231] Returns the serial number of a particular date in Microsoft excel

A] DATE

B] DATEVALUE

C] DAY

D] DAYS360

232] Converts a date in the form of text to a serial number in Microsoft excel

A] DATE

B] DATEVALUE

C] DAY

D] DAYS360

233] Converts a serial number to a day of the month in Microsoft excel

A] DATE

B] DATEVALUE

C] DAY

D] DAYS360

234] Calculates the number of days between two dates based on a 360-day year Microsoft excel

A] DATE

B] DATEVALUE

C] DAY

D] DAYS360

235] A PowerPoint presentation that you can create to display your personal or business photographs.

A] Photo album
B] Web presentation
C] Page orientation
D] Self-running presentation

236] which function is used in power point presentation to add information such as slide numbers, the time and date, a company logo, the presentation title or file name, the presenter's name, and more to the top of each handout or notes page in your presentation, or to bottom of each slide, handout or notes page

A] Slide number
B] Date & Time
C] Headers or Footers
D] Captions

237] Number slides from function at Quick Access Toolbar in Microsoft Power Point is used for

A] To change the slide number that appears on the first slide in your presentation

B] To change the slide number that appears on the last slide in your presentation

C] To change the slide number that appears on the middle slide in your presentation

D] To delete slide in your presentation

238] For creating email account one of below option is used

A] Log in
B] Sign in
C] Sign Up
D] Log out

239] Forgot password option is used for.....

A] Create new password
B] Edit password
C] Check validity of password
D] Verification of password

240] Compose tab is used in email account for

A] Delete email
B] Write new email
C] Import email
D] Export email

241] In email account unwanted emails are stored in this folder..

A] Sent

B] Spam

C] Trash

D] Drafts

242] If we send email to someone, copy of this email is saved in this folder...

A] Sent

B] Spam

C] Trash

D] Drafts

243] Deleted emails are saved in this folder...

A] Sent

B] Spam

C] Trash

D] Drafts

244] Incomplete emails are saved in this folder

A] Sent

B] Spam

C] Trash

D] Drafts

245] Option used for respond email.....

A] Forward

B] Reply

C] Print

D] Report Spam

246] Option for sending copy of received email.....

A] Forward

B] Reply

C] Print

D] Report Spam

9 798887 047072

Printed by Libri Plureos GmbH in Hamburg,
Germany